The Best Tales Ever Told
WARRIORS
& WITCHES

Written by Stewart Ross
Illustrated by Francis Phillipps

ALADDIN/WATTS
LONDON • SYDNEY

© Aladdin Books Ltd 1997

Designed and produced by
Aladdin Books Ltd
28 Percy Street
London W1P 0LD

ISBN 0 7496 3041 8(hb)
ISBN 0 7496 3606 8(pb)

First published in
Great Britain in 1997 by
Aladdin Books/Watts Books
96 Leonard Street
London EC2A 4RH

Editor
Jim Pipe

Designed by

David West • CHILDREN'S BOOKS
Designer
Simon Morse

Illustrated by
Francis Phillipps

Additional illustrations by
Ken Stott – B.L. Kearley

Language Consultant
Dr. Rhiannon Ash

Printed in Belgium
All rights reserved

A CIP catalogue record
for this book is available
from the British Library.

CONTENTS

MYTH MAGIC

HERE ARE FIFTEEN of the greatest and oldest tales ever told. The ancient Greeks began telling stories over 3,000 years ago, passing them on by word of mouth. Greek storytellers, called bards, travelled around the countryside telling tales of warriors, witches, gods and goddesses in long poems (*left*).

Later, the stories were written down, changed and added to. Then the Romans, who lived in Italy, conquered the Greeks and re-told their tales as well as making up new ones of their own. They renamed many of the Greek gods and heroes: Hercules, for example, is the Roman version of the Greek hero Herakles.

Myths tried to make sense of things people didn't understand. The Greeks told the Pandora myth, for instance, to explain why there was unhappiness in the world. Legends were based on things that actually happened. There was a time, for example, when there really was an ancient Troy. Later, storytellers created the legend of the wooden horse (*right*). Myths and legends usually had a moral – they tried to teach people how to behave. Their most obvious lesson was that only fools argued with the gods.

The tales of the Greeks and Romans changed a lot over the centuries. So you don't get confused, we have picked out the best bits and made them easy to understand. That way, we hope you'll enjoy them as much those who first heard them all those thousands of years ago.

A Beginner's Guide to Tongue-Twisting
The Greeks loved giving their heroes long, complicated names. To make it easier for you to say them, we have broken down all long names into words that you can recognise.

For example, "Polydectes" is polly-<u>deck</u>-tease. The underlining is to show you where to stress the word. So with Polydectes, say the <u>deck</u> a bit louder than the polly and the tease!

PANDORA *and the* JAR

I<small>N THE BEGINNING</small>, there were no people in the world. There were just gods and goddesses, and super-strong semi-gods and goddesses, called Titans. The two groups did not get on. The gods and goddesses, who lived on top of Mount Olympus, were clever, jealous and short-tempered. Down below, the Titans lumbered about looking for things to do.

A<small>fter</small> a while, a Titan named Prometheus (*pro-me-thee-us*) got bored with lumbering and took up clay modelling. His best models were human beings, who came to life. Prometheus liked them and gave them fire to cook with. To protect them, he also bottled up all the nasty things (such as bullying, telling lies and toothache) in a jar.

Gods vs Titans
The Greeks believed the gods and titans went on squabbling long after Pandora's time. They liked to paint pictures of them on their pots.

Z<small>eus</small>, the chief god, was not amused. He said fire was for gods, not people, and took it away again. Not to be outdone, Prometheus had a chat with the goddess of arts and crafts. She was so impressed by his smooth talk and rippling muscles that she let him climb Mount Olympus. There he stole a bit of smouldering charcoal from the fire god and brought it back to earth.

"Volcano" Comes from Vulcan
In Roman myth, the fire-god Vulcan worked as a blacksmith under a volcano on Vulcano, an island off the coast of Italy.

eople thought this was great, of course. Zeus didn't. Purple with rage, he plotted a terrible revenge. He made Pandora (*pan-door-ah*), an incredibly beautiful woman, and gave her to Prometheus' brother, Epimetheus (*ep-ee-mee-thee-us*). To begin with, Epimetheus couldn't believe his luck. Then he remembered Prometheus' warning never to accept anything from the gods, and with a sigh he turned Pandora down.

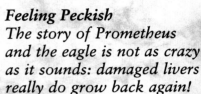

Feeling Peckish
The story of Prometheus and the eagle is not as crazy as it sounds: damaged livers really do grow back again!

This made Zeus even more furious. First, he had Prometheus chained to a mountain so he couldn't move. Then he got an eagle to fly up to the mountain every day and peck out his liver. At night, Zeus made the liver grow back again, so the torture could begin again in the morning – a warning for anyone who thought about messing with the gods.

Epimetheus got the message and married Pandora right away. This was just what Zeus had planned – he had made Pandora unbelievably stupid. Pottering about after breakfast one day, she came across Prometheus' jar and took out the cork to see what was inside.

Out zipped the nasties. They stung Pandora, Epimetheus and all the humans, making life on earth pretty miserable. But luckily Prometheus had also shoved Hope into the jar. It too escaped, so people believed one day things would get better. And that's how the world is today. The nastiness is still there, but we go on hoping it will go away.

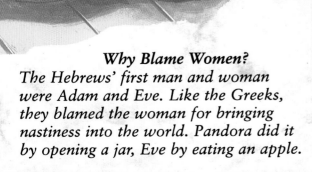

Why Blame Women?
The Hebrews' first man and woman were Adam and Eve. Like the Greeks, they blamed the woman for bringing nastiness into the world. Pandora did it by opening a jar, Eve by eating an apple.

ACHILLES' HEEL

ACHILLES' PARENTS WEREN'T LIKE OTHER PEOPLE'S. His dad was a warrior king and his mum was a sea nymph. So there wasn't much chance of Achilles (*ah-kill-ease*) turning out normal, either.

After nursing her baby for a bit, the nymph went back into the ocean. But before she left, she took Achilles to the magical River Styx that ran between the real world and the Underworld. Grabbing her son by his ankle, she dipped him into the dark waters. Achilles was too young to remember much. When he grew up, however, he realised something pretty amazing had happened. No weapon could harm him. Swords, spears and arrows all bounced off him and he became quite a warrior.

The Greeks' great enemies were the Trojans, from the distant city of Troy. One day, the word went round that Paris, a son of the Trojan king, had run off with a Greek woman. She was no ordinary woman, but Helen, the most beautiful woman in the world and wife of a Greek king. This was the last straw for the Greeks and, led by Agamemnon (*agg-ah-mem-non*), they set out for Troy in a huge fleet. After this, Helen was known as "the face that launched a thousand ships".

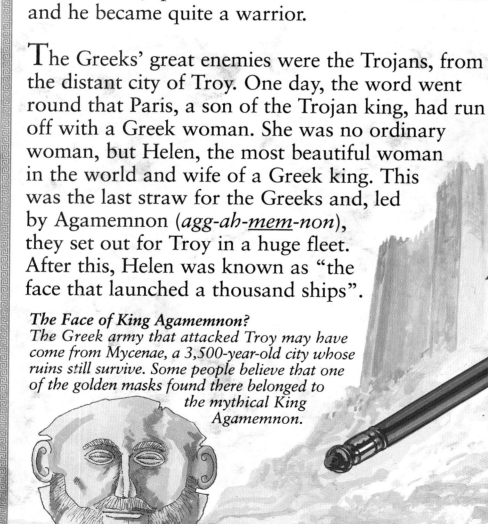

Greek Sing Along
*The story of Troy was first to[ld]
in long poems sung to music[.]
Later, they were written dou[wn]
by a blind poet named Hom[er.]*

The Face of King Agamemnon?
The Greek army that attacked Troy may have come from Mycenae, a 3,500-year-old city whose ruins still survive. Some people believe that one of the golden masks found there belonged to the mythical King Agamemnon.

Achilles soon followed, bringing his own army in sixty ships. On his journey he warmed up by attacking some of the Trojans' friends. After smashing up a town, he picked up a lovely girl who lived there and took her along with him. But when he got to Troy, the Greek leader Agamemnon took such a fancy to the girl that Achilles had to hand her over to him.

Helen the Cow?
Troy really did exist, but the Greeks probably attacked it to get back stolen cattle, not the beautiful Helen!

Achilles sulked. While the other Greeks were besieging Troy, he sat in his tent and refused to fight. He gave the job of leading his men to Patroclus (*pat-trok-luss*), his best friend. Some time later Patroclus was killed by Hector, another of the Trojan king's sons. When he heard about the death of his friend, Achilles roared into action. He chased Hector round the walls, caught him, hacked him to death and dragged his body behind his chariot.

Achilles the Greek super-hero was now Trojan enemy no. 1. Paris armed himself with a special bow and poisoned arrows and came looking for him. When the two met, Paris raised his bow and fired. Achilles just stood there and grinned, believing no weapon could hurt him.

He was wrong. The arrow stuck in the heel his mother had held him by. It was the only part of his body that had not been dipped in the Styx. Too late he realised his weakness, and within a few minutes he was dead.

Medical Myth
Doctors today call the tendon at the back of the foot the "Achilles tendon". And we call someone's weak point their "Achilles' heel".

CIRCE *the* WITCH

THANKS TO THE WILY HERO Odysseus, (*oh-dee-see-us*) the Greeks captured Troy and trashed it. They then held a wild party to celebrate, packed their bags and set off home.

The Odyssey
The story of Odysseus' wandering is known as the "Odyssey", a wor we use today for any long and dangerous voyage.

Odysseus, who hadn't seen his wife Penelope for ages, was one of the first to leave. But he ran into all sorts of trouble and instead of 10 days, the trip took 10 years. Soon after leaving, he had a really gruesome time in Sicily, where a gang of flesh-eating giants sank eleven of his twelve ships and ate the crews.

Were Monsters
There are many stories of humans changing into animals. Europeans feared werewolves, Africans believed in wereleopards and weretigers were said to prowl all over Asia.

Happy to get away in one piece, he made for the lush-looking Isle of Dawn. The place seemed peaceful enough, so he decided to stay a few days to get over the nightmare of the monster meat-eaters. But he was taking no chances. He stayed behind to guard the ships and sent the captain and his men to check the place out.

Wandering inland, they came across a palace surrounded by animals – dogs, foxes, lions and so on – all standing on their hind legs. To their amazement, the beasts bounced up and greeted them in a really friendly way. Then a beautiful woman came out and invited everyone in for a meal. Hardly believing their good luck, the sailors trooped indoors.

But the captain smelt a rat and hung back. Just as well, too. Peering round the door, he saw all his crew turned into pigs. As they trotted off to join the other animals, he sprinted back to the beach to warn his leader.

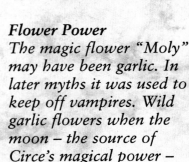

Odysseus realised he couldn't get away without a crew and set off to rescue them. On the way he bumped into the god Hermes, who warned him that the woman was Circe (*sir-see*), a sort of goddess-witch. To ward off her magic, Hermes gave Odysseus a special scented flower, known as Moly.

Flower Power
The magic flower "Moly" may have been garlic. In later myths it was used to keep off vampires. Wild garlic flowers when the moon – the source of Circe's magical power – looks smallest in the sky.

Circe was a real stunner. She charmed Odysseus with her magic and got ready to piggify him. He sniffed his Moly in the nick of time, then grabbed his sword and threatened to kill her. Thinking fast, Circe tried more female charms.

"Honey," she smiled, "I'll give you *anything* you want, as long as you spare my life." Odysseus looked at her. "Fine," he agreed, "but only if you turn all these animals back into people." As Circe rather fancied him, she accepted his offer.

Odysseus and his new girlfriend got on really well, but he still missed Penelope. In the end, he left the island and, after many more adventures, finally made it home.

Magic Mum
Circe was daughter of Hecate, goddess of the moon. Many ancient people linked the moon with magic because of the mysterious way it affected the tides.

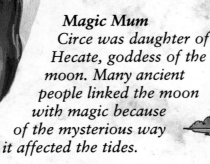

AENEAS *and the* GOLDEN BRANCH

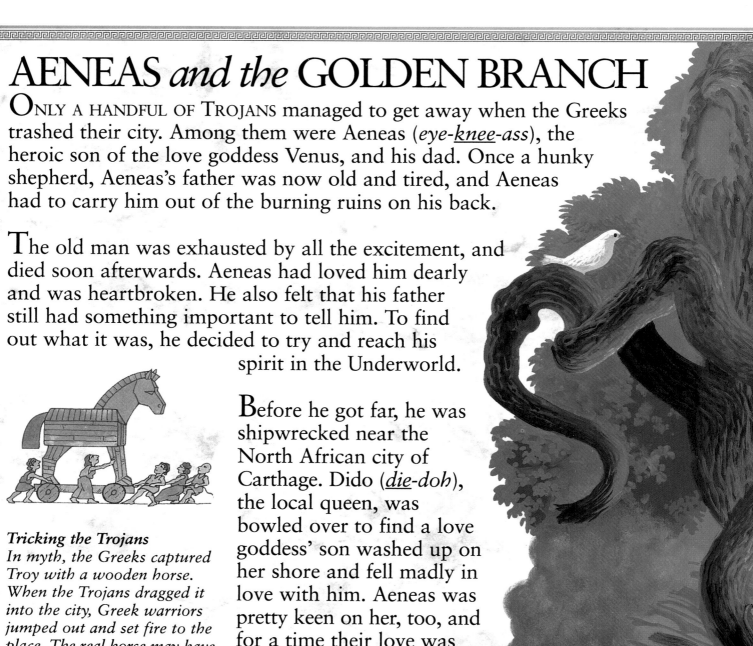

Oɴʟʏ ᴀ ʜᴀɴᴅғᴜʟ ᴏғ Tʀᴏᴊᴀɴs managed to get away when the Greeks trashed their city. Among them were Aeneas (*eye-knee-ass*), the heroic son of the love goddess Venus, and his dad. Once a hunky shepherd, Aeneas's father was now old and tired, and Aeneas had to carry him out of the burning ruins on his back.

The old man was exhausted by all the excitement, and died soon afterwards. Aeneas had loved him dearly and was heartbroken. He also felt that his father still had something important to tell him. To find out what it was, he decided to try and reach his spirit in the Underworld.

Tricking the Trojans
In myth, the Greeks captured Troy with a wooden horse. When the Trojans dragged it into the city, Greek warriors jumped out and set fire to the place. The real horse may have been a giant battering ram!

Before he got far, he was shipwrecked near the North African city of Carthage. Dido (*die-doh*), the local queen, was bowled over to find a love goddess' son washed up on her shore and fell madly in love with him. Aeneas was pretty keen on her, too, and for a time their love was the hottest thing in Africa.

Sadly, the gods had other plans for Aeneas. They didn't want him growing old in Dido's arms, however comfortable that might be, and they told him to leave. Being half god himself, Aeneas knew better than to argue and he sailed off into the sunset. Poor Dido was so upset, she killed herself.

Aeneas' next stop was Italy. Here, in a dark, smoky cave, lived a Sibyl (*si-bull*), a shrivelled old crone with the power to see into the future.

The crafty prophetess told him he would be allowed into the Underworld only if he took a present for Proserpina (*pro-sir-pee-na*), Queen of the Underworld. "What sort of present?" Aeneas asked. The Sibyl replied that what the queen really craved was not flowers or chocolates, but a golden branch.

The City of Carthage
The real city of Carthage was on the coast of North Africa, and was one of ancient Rome's toughest enemies. Its most famous leader was Hannibal, who attacked the Romans with elephants in his army.

Aeneas wandered about for ages looking for a tree with a shiny sprig. Finally, guided by a couple of helpful doves, he found the right sort of branch, snapped it off and took the path to the murky depths. Although Dido's ghost wasn't too pleased to see him again, the gleaming twig was just what Proserpine had always wanted and she gave him permission to chat with his dead dad.

Now he was a ghost, the old man knew just about everything: past, present and future. Aeneas listened in wonder as the spirit told him that he – Aeneas – would set up the greatest empire ever!

Knowing what he had to do, Aeneas itched to get on with it. He clambered back up to the surface and, after more adventures, arrived on the banks of the River Tiber in Italy. Here he became King of the Latins and set up the Roman Empire – just as his dad had prophesied.

Who Can Tell?
The Romans longed to see into the future. They used all sorts of ways, such as studying the flight of birds, or staring at the guts of dead animals.

ROMULUS *builds a* CITY

THE TEMPLE OF THE FIRESIDE GOD was looked after by young women called the Vestal Virgins. They had a really good life, as long as they didn't go out with men. So when Rhea Silva, one of the Virgins, got pregnant and gave birth to twin boys, she was in deep trouble.

Still Going Strong
Some ancient gods and goddesses (e.g. Mars, Venus and Mercury) are still with as the names of the planets in our solar system.

To everyone's amazement, she explained that the boys' father was not a man but Mars, the god of war. Some believed her, but not the king. After locking her in prison, he put the twins, Romulus (*rom-mule-us*) and Remus (*ree-mus*), in a basket and floated it out onto the River Tiber.

Brother Bashing
Romulus wasn't the only murderous brother in ancient times. In the Bible, Cain carries out the first murder by bashing his brother Abel with a stone.

As far as the king was concerned, that was the end of Romulus and Remus. But it's not that easy to kill a god's children. The basket drifted a long way downstream and came ashore on a sloping bank. Here a she-wolf found it and carefully carried the babies off to her cave. Living off the wolf's milk, they grew strong and lively.

A few months later, a shepherd whose flock had been attacked by the wolf went looking for her. The beast heard him coming and scuttled off into the woods, leaving the twins behind. The abandoned boys kicked up a terrible din.

he shepherd soon found the two babies and took them home. In me, he and his wife discovered who the boys were and, when ey were grown up, told them about their parents and their icked uncle. The story filled Romulus and Remus with fury. hey stormed down to the town, drove out the king and decided set up a city of their own.

omulus, the more hard-working of the two, drew up ans and set to work. Remus thought his brother's design as lousy. "Your weedy walls wouldn't keep out a half-ead sheep," he teased, "let alone an invading army". omulus ignored him and went on building.

Wife Snatching
The early Romans found themselves short of women. They solved the problem by inviting the local Sabine men to a party. Meanwhile, the Romans raided the Sabine HQ and carried off all the women they could lay their hands on.

When the walls were up to his waist, Remus was still making nasty comments. By this time, Romulus, all hot and sweaty with the work he had done, was starting to get annoyed. Then, to show how useless the walls were, Remus ran up and jumped over them.

hariot of Fire
hen Romulus died, he was hisked off to heaven in a fiery ariot to become the god Quirinus.

This was more than Romulus could take. As Remus landed, his brother thumped him with a spade and killed him. After burying the body, he went on with his work and soon finished the city. He named it after himself, of course, not his annoying brother, and it is still called "Rome" today.

The GOLDEN FLEECE

KING PELIAS (_pelly-ass_) WAS A NASTY piece of work. He had stolen his kingdom and wiped out anyone who said it wasn't rightfully his. His only worry was a prophesy that someone with one shoe would kill him. So he was a bit jittery when one day a young man with a sandal missing limped into court.

Horsemen
Centaurs were half-man, half-horse. The myth probably came from Thessaly, in central Greece, where the riders were so good they seemed joined to their horses.

This was Jason, who had lost his sandal crossing a river. He was the true king, he said, and had come to get his crown. Pelias thought hard and fast. Sure, he agreed, Jason could have his crown – as long as he got hold of some famous shiny wool known as the Golden Fleece.

Jason, who loved adventure, accepted Pelias' challenge. He collected a band of warriors and set sail in the _Argo_ to find the Fleece. As with all heroes in those times, Jason and his mates (the Argonauts) had a tough time getting anywhere. But after all sorts of problems they reached the city of Colchis (_koll-kiss_) near where the Fleece was kept.

The Oracle Speaks
The most popular way to find out what was going to happen in the ancient world was to ask the oracle at Delphi in Greece. But its crafty answers always had more than one meaning.

The King of Colchis said that Jason could have the Fleece if he passed a simple test. All he had to do was yoke a couple of fire-breathing bulls, plough a field with them and then sow it with dragons' teeth, which would turn into an army of soldiers!

ason was just about to give up and go home when the king's daughter, Medea (*med-dee-err*), sidled up to him and offered to help. Medea was really attractive, of course. She was also a witch, which meant she was good at spells. Even better, she had fallen madly in love with the dashing Jason and was willing to do anything to help him.

Thanks to Medea's magic, Jason managed the ploughing and sowing. And when the army of soldiers burst out of the ground, he even tricked them into fighting each other. But when he asked for the Fleece, Medea's dad changed his mind and said it wasn't going anywhere.

Look Out
"Dragon" may come from the Greek word drakon, *meaning to watch. Greek dragons are usually sharp-eyed monster-guards, while dragons in Far Eastern myths are more gentle creatures.*

Once again, Medea came to the rescue. She showed Jason where the fleece was and put to sleep the dragon that guarded it. Before the king could stop him, Jason grabbed his woolly prize and sprinted back to the *Argo* with it. Medea came aboard too, determined not to lose her man.

The story might have ended happily after all this, but it didn't. Jason got his kingdom back and Medea, showing her nasty side, had ex-King Pelias boiled alive. Jason then left her for another woman and she went crazy with rage.

Not long afterwards, the Argonauts pulled their ship onto the beach and their leader lay down in its shade for a snooze. He never woke up. When a bit of the boat fell off and killed him, even Jason's amazing luck had finally run out.

Ship Shape
In Greek myth, the Argo *was the first long ship. Real ships in ancient Greece were also long, narrow and powered by sails and rows of oars.*

HERCULES *and the* AMAZONS

HERCULES, SON OF ZEUS, looked like the ultimate mega-hero. His muscles swelled like lead-filled balloons and he was as brave as a lioness. But looks aren't everything. He had a sharp temper and an even sharper eye for the women. This annoyed the jealous goddess Hera and she gave him a fit of madness in which he killed his children.

King Skin
After killing the Nemean Lion, Hercules wore its skin as a cloak. A lion's skin has been worn by many kings as a sign of power.

To earn forgiveness, Hercules agreed to serve the local king for twelve years. The old man didn't want the beefy brute hanging about court, so he sent him on twelve really dangerous missions. Most involved killing monsters of some sort, but the ninth mission was different. "Find Hippolyta (*hip-poll-i-tah*), the Queen of the Amazons, and bring back her belt for my daughter," the king commanded.

This wasn't as easy as it sounded. The Amazons were a tribe of fierce warrior women, famous for burning off their right breasts to make them better archers. Hippolyta, daughter of the war god Mars and as tough as she was beautiful, would *not* appreciate a stranger fiddling about with her clothes.

Women Warriors
The mythical Amazons may be based on the Scythians, a tribe in Asia Minor whose women fought alongside the men.

To begin with, things went better than Hercules dared hope. Hippolyta was so taken by his bulging body that she couldn't wait to give him her belt – and any other bit of her dress he wanted. Unfortunately for Hercules, when Hera heard of the handsome hunk's hanky-panky, she dressed as an Amazon and went to put a stop to it.

While Hercules and Hippolyta were giggling in her tent, Hera set about stirring up trouble among the Amazons. "Hercules is up to no good," she hissed. "Don't trust him. It's not really the belt he wants – he's going to run off with your queen!"

Bulging Belts
Belts were signs of power – but not for Scotland's King James IV. He wore a heavy iron belt, adding an extra chunk each year, to remind him that he had fought against his father.

As Hera had planned, this made the Amazons really furious. Grabbing their weapons, they burst in on the queen and her playmate. "Fool!" they screamed, "You starry-eyed dreamer, get real! Can't you see what's happening? You're betraying us for the sake of this no-good mound of muscle."

Hippolyta had to choose in an instant between Hercules and her loyal women. Being a good queen at heart, she sided with her own kind and, in next to no time, an almighty fight had broken out. The Amazons didn't stand a chance against Hercules' brute force. He easily ripped off Hippolyta's belt and, leaving the queen and her Amazons in a battered heap, trotted happily back home to see if the king could find something *really* difficult for him to do.

Break Out
The ancients said the Mediterranean was cut off from the Atlantic until Hercules forced his way through. Afterwards, the rocks of the Straits of Gibraltar were known as the Pillars of Hercules.

HERCULES *and* the WATCH DOG

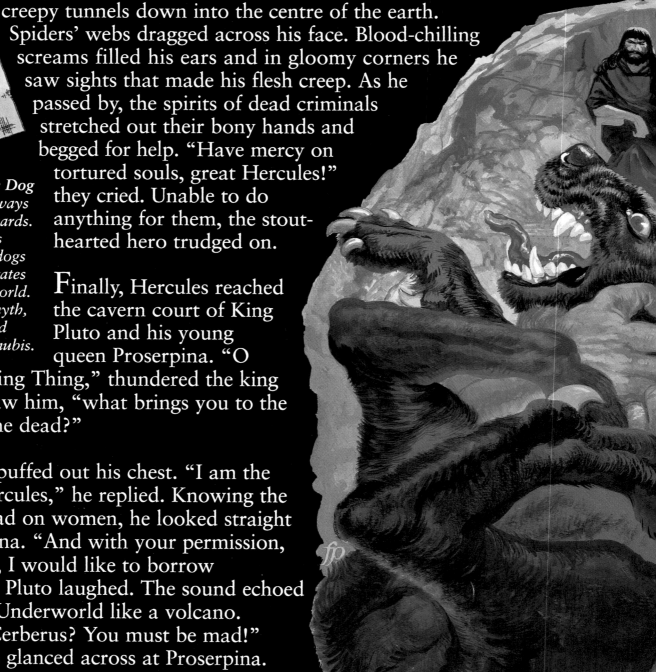

H ERCULES' LAST MISSION was the most difficult of the lot. He had to visit the fearful Underworld and bring back the flesh-tearing Cerberus (*sir-berr-us*). This was a huge, three-headed dog whose razor-sharp fangs guarded the entrance to the Underworld.

Tantalising Torture
In the Underworld Hercules met Tantalus, who was tortured by thi and hunger for telling th gods' secrets. He stood t to his neck in water, bu every time he bent dow to drink, it vanished. Above him, just out of reach, hung bunches of fruit. His punishment gi us the word "tantalise"

U sing his skills as a hunter, Hercules followed the creepy tunnels down into the centre of the earth. Spiders' webs dragged across his face. Blood-chilling screams filled his ears and in gloomy corners he saw sights that made his flesh creep. As he passed by, the spirits of dead criminals stretched out their bony hands and begged for help. "Have mercy on tortured souls, great Hercules!" they cried. Unable to do anything for them, the stout-hearted hero trudged on.

Beware of the Dog
Dogs have always made good guards. Many ancients believed that dogs stood by the gates of the spirit world. In Egyptian myth, the dog-headed guardian is Anubis.

F inally, Hercules reached the cavern court of King Pluto and his young queen Proserpina. "O foolish Living Thing," thundered the king when he saw him, "what brings you to the world of the dead?"

T he hero puffed out his chest. "I am the mighty Hercules," he replied. Knowing the effect he had on women, he looked straight at Proserpina. "And with your permission, noble king, I would like to borrow Cerberus." Pluto laughed. The sound echoed round the Underworld like a volcano. "Borrow Cerberus? You must be mad!" Then Pluto glanced across at Proserpina.

What do you think, Light of my Darkness?" If the queen had been able to blush, she would have done. "He must be brave to come down here all alone," she gasped. "So he wants to borrow the hound, why not?". "Very well," Pluto agreed, "you may borrow Cerberus. But only if you catch him with your bare hands and bring him back when you have finished with him."

Hercules thanked them and went off to tackle the triple-awed monster. The beast was pretty terrifying, but Hercules was not going to be beaten now. Pluto looked on as Hercules dodged the foaming fangs, grasped the dog round two of its mangy necks and strangled them. Left with only one working head, Cerberus calmed down and followed them meekly up to the surface.

Furious Ladies
In Greek myth, three merciless Furies – who give us the words "fury" and "furious" – were in charge of punishing wrongdoers.

When Hercules' mission master saw the dog, he ran screaming from his court and was never seen again. The hero's tasks were now over. True to his word, he took Cerberus back to the Underworld. A little later, after still more amazing feats, the gods invited Hercules to join them on Mount Olympus. He gladly accepted and back on earth, a lot of monsters and villains were mighty relieved to see the back of him.

Springtime in Ancient Greece
Proserpine was the only bright spot in the Underworld. She didn't like living with Pluto and returned to the world for half a year. The Greeks believed her annual trip to the surface marked the beginning of spring.

ORPHEUS *and* EURYDICE

THE GOD APOLLO DISHED out talents to the people he liked. To Orpheus (*oar-fee-us*), his favourite, he gave the gifts of poetry and music, making him the greatest poet and musician ever. He was never stuck for a rhyme. When he played his lyre, wild beasts became tame and trees pulled up their roots to dance.

Once Bitten
Snakes, which crop up in many legends, are both holy and wicked. The most famous evil snake was sent by the devil to tempt Eve in the Garden of Eden.

As a young man, Orpheus sailed with Jason's Argonauts. When the *Argo* got back with the Golden Fleece, he fell in love with a lovely nymph named Euridice (*your-rid-ee-see*). They were soon married and for a few months were extremely happy.

Unknown to Orpheus, a lusty beekeeper was also crazy about Euridice. One evening, when Orpheus was away playing at a party and Euridice was strolling by the river, he crept up on her. Euridice saw him just in time and ran off, with the beekeeper in hot pursuit. Unfortunately, she didn't look where she was going and trod on a snake. The creature reared up and bit her on the leg. Within a few minutes she was dead.

When he returned and found out what had happened, Orpheus was so unhappy he almost gave up playing for good. But he pulled himself together and decided to use his talent to try and get Euridice back from the Underworld.

Musical Fare
The ferryman Charon gave Orpheus a free passage across the River Styx because he played so well. The Greeks thought music was so important that they made it a key subject at school.

...wanging away on his lyre, Orpheus gingerly entered ...e gloomy tunnels. The effect of his music was ...mazing! Cerberus stopped growling and sat wagging ...is tail in time to the beat. The spirits of the dead forgot ...heir misery and joined in the chorus. Even Pluto and ...roserpine were impressed and danced a few steps together.

...hey hadn't enjoyed themselves so much for years, they said, and of course Orpheus could take Euridice back to the surface. But on one condition: he must not look back at her until they were both in the sunlight.

Greek Heaven and Hell
The Underworld wasn't all gloom and doom. The Greeks thought it had three parts: Tartarus (the hellish bit), where baddies were tortured, the Land of Shadows, where most people went, and the Elysian Fields, the heavenly bit where great heroes enjoyed themselves.

So off Orpheus went, playing away for all he was worth. Following the sound, his beloved Euridice tagged along a few yards behind. Up, up they went, until Orpheus felt the sun on the back of his neck once more. Thinking Euridice was hot on his heels, he stopped playing and turned to grab her. But she was still in shadow! As she fell back into the darkness, Orpheus knew that just one silly mistake had cost him a lifetime of happiness.

Party God
The Greek god Dionysus (die-oh-nice-us) was a great music lover. The drunken parties held in his honour, where excited women danced in the woods, were the beginnings of ancient Greek theatre.

THESEUS *and the* MINOTAUR

Bull Jumping
The Minotaur didn't exist, but the ancient Cretans were mad about bulls. Boys and girls took part in a crazy sport where they vaulted on and off the snorting beasts.

THESEUS WAS THE TOP hero of the city of Athens. Like most heroes, he had bulging muscles and performed incredible feats of strength, bravery and so on. His most famous deed was killing the horrible maze-monster of Crete.

Theseus' dad, King Aegeus (*eye-gee-us*) of Athens, was seriously hassled by King Minos, a black-bearded bully from Crete who collected unusual pets. The oddest was the Minotaur, a revolting bull-headed monster that lived in a maze and ate nothing but humans.

Unwilling to feed the Minotaur with Cretans, Minos ordered his monster munch from Aegeus. Athens had to send a regular flesh supply, Minos warned, or he would sail over and trash the place. So from time to time, seven young men and seven young women were shipped from Athens to Crete to feed the Minotaur.

The Amazing Maze
The maze in the Minotaur story may be based on the real palace at Knossos in Crete, which had dozens of rooms and passages.

Theseus decided to put a stop to this and volunteered as a victim. Normally, all ships returning from Crete had black sails. Before leaving, Theseus told Aegeus that if he succeeded, he would return flying a white sail.

Minos took an instant dislike to Theseus: the young Athenian was too handsome and confident for his liking. The Cretan women, however, thought he was a knockout. To Minos' daughter, Ariadne (*arry-add-knee*), he was the coolest thing since the Ice Age and she offered to help him slay the Minotaur if he took her back to Athens afterwards. Theseus loved the idea of killing the monster and getting a scorching new girlfriend, so he agreed.

That night Ariadne gave Theseus a ball of magic string and let him into the maze. As he moved through the dark passages, he let out the string behind him. At the centre he found the Minotaur – all froth and roar and stamping – and killed him. Then, following the string back to the entrance, he collected Ariadne and ran back to his ship.

The other victims joined him and soon they were all skimming back to Athens. Unfortunately, the god Dionysus (*die-oh-nice-us*) also fancied Ariadne, so when the Athenians stopped at an island to pick up water, he put a memory-loss spell on Theseus.

Unable to remember who Ariadne was, the hero left without her. Dionysus moved in like a shot and married her before she worked out what was going on.

When his memory came back, Theseus was so upset at losing Ariadne that he stupidly forgot about the white sail. Aegeus, watching from a cliff, saw his son's ship with a black sail and threw himself into the sea (*right*). This ruined Theseus' homecoming and, to remind him of his poor drowned dad, he named the sea the Aegean.

ICARUS' WINGS

NOT ALL GREEK HEROES were big-bodied bruisers. Daedalus (_die-dah-luss_), for example, was quite a weedy little man, but his brain was the envy of everyone. It was simply the sharpest and biggest ever and Daedalus used it to invent useful things, such as the saw and the axe.

When Minos wanted somewhere to keep his Minotaur, he sent for Daedalus. The genius thought for a few seconds, then came up with the idea of the maze. It was so clever that Minos didn't want anyone else to have one, so he refused to let Daedalus leave Crete.

Big Thinkers
The ancient Greeks were brilliant at maths and science. They worked out the rules of geometry, why ships float, and even how to make steam engines and simple calculators!

The inventor's son Icarus (_ik-ah-russ_), who had come along for a holiday, was quite upset when he heard they weren't allowed home. Daedalus scratched his head. "Don't worry, son. I'll think of something."

Sun Worship
The early Greeks worshipped the sun-god Helios. They believed he lit the world by driving his fiery chariot across the sky.

He drew up plans, then went down to the shops and came back with some wax and a couple of sacks of feathers. "What are you up to, dad?" Icarus asked. "Wait and see," muttered Daedalus, tipping out the feathers onto the floor and starting to sort through them. Icarus went outside to sunbathe.

A week later Daedalus' latest invention was ready. He called Icarus in and showed him four huge feathery things propped up against the wall.

All in a Flap
Five hundred years ago, a man tried flying off the walls of Stirling Castle in Scotland. He went straight down and fell in a dung heap. This was hardly surprising. To fly using only our arms, we would need muscles as big as a horse's.

"What on earth are they?" he asked in amazement. "Wings!" cried the brain-box. "We're going home by air!"

That afternoon, they took the wings and climbed to the top of a hill. "You sure they'll work, dad?" Icarus asked nervously as he strapped the contraptions onto his arms

"Work? Of course they'll work! But don't fly too near the sun. If you do, the wax will melt and the feathers will fall out. You'll end up in the drink!"

Minutes later, flapping and shouting, the inventor and his son took off. Flying was hard work at first and Icarus almost nose-dived into a house. But by watching the seagulls they soon got the hang of things and headed out to sea. "This is great!" yelled Icarus as he soared higher. "I can see for miles!" "Don't forget what I told you," warned Daedalus, who was skimming along just above the waves.

The foolish boy was now no more than a speck in the sky. "What did you say, dad? Speak up!" "I said don't forget…" It was no use. The wax in Icarus' wings melted and he tumbled headlong into the sea and drowned. After circling the spot for a few minutes, Daedalus flapped his arms and finished the sad flight home by himself.

Sun and Sacrifice
Because the Sun's rays make life on Earth possible, it's not surprising that many ancient peoples worshipped it. The Aztecs sacrificed thousands of victims each year to feed their sun god.

MARATHON MAN

THE PEOPLE OF GREECE were incredibly sporty. They spent all their spare time running, jumping and throwing things, and once every four years they went to an Olympic Games to see who were the best athletes. But the Games had only sprint races, so long distance runners never became famous. This really cheesed them off.

Pigeon Power
In ancient times, messages were carried by pigeons, as well as by horseriders and runners. The Greeks used pigeons to report winners from the Olympic games.

One Athenian runner was more cheesed off than most because he reckoned he was the fittest Greek of the lot. Sadly, as he never had a chance to prove it, no one took much notice of him. Until the Persians arrived.

Persian Peril
The Persians tried several times to conquer Greece. The Battle of Marathon was fought in 490 BC, when King Darius I invaded.

The Persian army was the biggest and best in the world, with cavalry that made mincemeat of everyone that got in its way. After landing on the beach at Marathon, just north of Athens, the Persians set up camp and waited for the Greeks to come, so they could show them who was boss.

Although the Athenian foot soldiers were pretty good, because their cavalry was lousy they didn't reckon they had much chance. They were not cowards, however, and all of them, including the cheesed off runner, went up to Marathon prepared to do their best.

Peace and Riches
The city of Athens was named after the goddess Athene. In myth she offered it an olive branch, a sign of peace and riches.

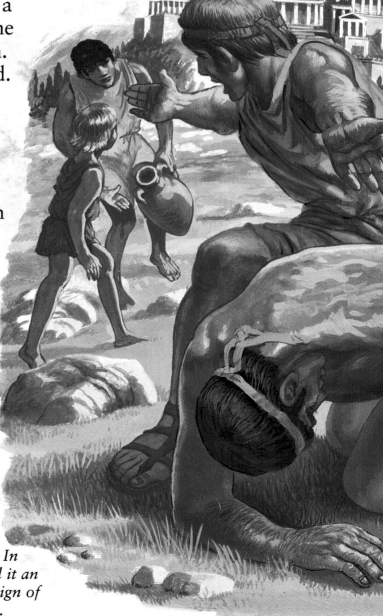

Luckily, just after the Athenians arrived the Persian cavalry had a day off. This was the chance the Athenians needed. They leaped from behind their defences and sprinted like crazy towards the enemy, who were still having breakfast. The Persians were in no mood to fight and those who were not killed pelted back to their ships. When the cavalry turned up a few hours later, the battle was already over.

The Olympic Games
The Greeks set up the Olympics in honour of the chief god Zeus. They were held every four years from 776 BC to 392 AD, but there were no long distance races.

It was the greatest victory Athens had ever won. Although the proud general was keen to get news of it back to the city as quickly as possible, his soldiers were too shattered to move, let alone run back to Athens. Then, to everyone's amazement, up jumped the runner, who wanted so much to be famous. "I'll go!" he cried.

So off he went. It's about 42 kilometres from Marathon to Athens and by half way the messenger was so puffed he could hardly run. But he bravely kept going until he finally staggered into the city, where he collapsed in a heap.

"We've won!" he gasped. "We've beaten the Persians." But the citizens were so busy shouting and cheering at the great news they forgot to ask the runner's name. When someone finally remembered and returned to find out, it was too late. He was dead.

We still don't know who the runner was. But today 42-kilometre marathon races are held in his honour all over the world – so he has become famous after all.

MIDAS' GOLDEN TOUCH

KING MIDAS JUST *LOVED* PLEASURE. Harps played wherever he went, gooey-eyed maidens scrubbed his back when he took a bath – and he always had breakfast in bed. What he enjoyed best, however, was the scent of roses. So he could always smell their perfume, his palace was surrounded by rose gardens, stretching as far as the eye could see.

Boozy Beasts
Satyrs, half-man, half-animal, were famous for drinking wine and having a laugh. Early Greek comedies were called Satyr plays because the Satyrs in them poked fun at the grand heroes on stage.

One day, a gardener came running in from the furthest flower bed to say he had found a strange creature lurking there. Midas, who was keen on curiosities, went to look for himself. To his surprise he found an old satyr (<u>sat</u>-err) – half-goat, half-man – asleep under a rose bush.

Money Man
Mythical Midas was king of Phrygia. This was a real country where some of the first coins were made.

Satyrs were the jolly but rather wicked servants of the party god Dionysus. This one, Silenus (<u>sy</u>-<u>lean</u>-uss), had wandered into the garden after an all-night rave and collapsed. Midas approved of Dionysus – a god after his own heart – and treated Silenus very kindly. He fed him well and even allowed his gooey-eyed maidens to scrub his hairy back. As soon as the satyr was feeling better, he set off to find his master. Midas who had never seen a god, tagged along too.

Dionysus was delighted to see Silenus again. And when he heard how well Midas had treated him, as a reward he granted the king one wish. "Just say the word," he smiled, "and it will be yours!" "Anything I want?" gasped Midas. "Great!" Without thinking he said "I wish that everything I touch turns to gold." "Your wish is granted," said the god. "Now off you go and enjoy it!"

The Gleaming King
The Muisca people of South America were also fascinated by gold. So their king could salute the sun god, they showered his body in gold dust to make him a "golden man".

Grinning all over his face, Midas walked towards the palace. He put out his hand to touch a rose. Zap! It turned to gold. "Wow!" he cried. "I'm the richest king in the world!" He put his hand in his pocket to get a sweet. But it tasted foul and broke a tooth when he tried to bite it. By evening he realised he had made a terrible mistake. His food, his drink, even his favourite daughter were all solid gold.

Starving hungry, he went off to tell Dionysus what was happening. The god was not surprised. "You greedy man," he sighed. "I hope you've learned your lesson. Now go and wash in the spring that feeds the River Pactolus (*pack-toe-luss*)."

Holy Dip
Water has a special place in most religions. Just as the river washed away Midas' greed, so Christians and Hindus bathe to wash away their sins.

Midas thanked him and hurried off to the spring. The moment the water sloshed over him, the spell was broken. Everything he had touched changed back again. But Dionysus had taught him a useful lesson and he was never quite so keen on gold again…

PERSEUS *and the* GORGONS

PERSEUS (*percy-us*) HAD AN UNHAPPY CHILDHOOD. Although his dad was the King of the Gods, Zeus, he didn't see much of him and was brought up in the court of bullying King Polydectes (*polly-deck-tease*). What made Perseus really upset was the way the king leered at his mother. When Perseus' mum said she didn't want anything to do with Polydectes, he changed tactics. He was going to marry another woman, he lied, and asked his friends for unusual wedding presents. This set Perseus thinking.

The next day Polydectes asked Perseus what he was going to give him. "Something really special," the lad replied. "Oh yes?" smirked the king. "What?" Perseus looked him straight in the eye. "I'm going to fetch you the head of Medusa (*med-use-ah*)," he said quietly.

Priestess Power
The story of the female Gorgons may come from very early on in Greek history, when priestesses worshipped the moon. Later, invaders forced them out and introduced a sun religion run by men.

Medusa was a Gorgon, one of three foul women with iron teeth, huge claws and snakes instead of hair. They were so hideous that anyone who looked at them turned to stone.

Polydectes roared with laughter. "Great idea, Perseus!" Medusa's head is just what I need. Please go and fetch it." It was the surest way he knew of getting rid of the annoying young man for ever.

Medusa was really unpopular. When the goddess Athene heard of Perseus' plan, she explained how to tell Medusa apart from the other Gorgons and gave him a shield polished on one side like a mirror. Other enemies of Medusa [fi]tted him out with a razor-sharp sickle, sandals with [w]ings, a magic bag and a helmet that made him invisible.

Basket Babes
As a baby, Perseus was set adrift at sea in a chest. The most famous floating baby was Moses, who was put in a basket to save him from the Egyptians.

Carrying all this gear, Perseus made his way to the Gorgons' lair and slipped on his winged sandals. Then, looking in the shield to see where he was going, he flew inside, picked out Medusa and sliced off her head with the sickle.

[Th]ree Gorgons, Wise Men, Little Pigs...
[In] myth, three is a special number. The ancient Greek [m]athematician Pythagoras said it was holy, because [it] stood for the beginning, the middle and the end.

When an armed soldier and the flying horse Pegasus sprang up out of her dead body, Perseus decided it was time to get out – fast. He popped Medusa's head into the bag and, pulling the invisibility helmet over his head, vanished in the nick of time.

Just as Polydectes was telling everyone they had seen the last of Perseus, in he walked carrying the bag. The king turned white. "G-g-got the head, sonny?" he stammered. "Sure," Perseus smiled. "Want to see it?"

Polydectes looked scornfully at the bag. "You haven't got Medusa's head, you wimp! A goat's head, more likely!" They were the last words he ever spoke. Glancing away, Perseus drew out his dripping prize and turned the bullying king and his courtiers to statues.

The FLYING HORSE

THE QUEEN OF TIRYNS was bored. She was bored with silly courtiers, bored with her clothes and, above all, bored with her unbelievably dull husband, the king.

So when one day a handsome young warrior turned up at court, she made straight for him, threw her arms around his neck and whispered in his ear "Cheer me up, stranger!"

Gifted Horses
Horses were a favourite gift in the ancient world. The Romans sacrificed the leading horse of a winning chariot race team to Mars, the god of war.

The warrior, whose name was Bellerophon (*bell-lair-oh-phone*), was far too polite to go along with this sort of thing. He carefully took the queen's arms from his shoulders and explained that he liked her a lot – but not that much.

Steaming with fury, the queen ran to her husband. "King!" she screamed. "That puppy Bellerophon has just been incredibly rude to me. Cut off his head, right now!" The king was too weedy to do the queen's dirty work himself. He sent Bellerophon to his father-in-law Iobates (*yo-bait-ease*) and asked him to kill the young man.

Mix-and-Match Monster
nother strange beast in
reek myth is the griffon,
ith an eagle's head and
ings and a lion's body.

All-in-One Enemy
The mythical Chimera was all dangers and
seasons rolled into one. The story may be
based on an old ritual. To show their power,
ancient kings had pretend fights with men
dressed as a lion (spring), a goat (summer)
and a snake (winter).

But Iobates felt sorry for
Bellerophon and, instead of murdering him in cold blood,
he asked him to go and kill the Chimera (kye-_mare_-rah).
This was almost the same as murder, because the
Chimera was a fire-breathing monster that burned to
a cinder everyone who came near it.

Bellerophon was certainly *not*
weedy and he accepted Iobates'
challenge without hesitating.
The first thing he did, never
having hunted a flame-throwing
part-lion, part-goat, part-serpent
before, was ask around for advice.
His best chance, he was told, lay
in an air attack from the back of a
flying horse.

Holy and Horrible Horses
Mythology is full of weird
horses, such as the horned
unicorn, Viking god Odin's
eight-legged horse, the
holy horse of Gaul, water
horses, meat-eating horses
and, of course, the
wooden horse
of Troy.

Bellerophon knew of
only one flying horse.
This was Pegasus, the
noble beast who had flown out of
Medusa's neck when her head was cut
off. Bellerophon found out where the
creature lived and went off to catch it.

After several tries, he slipped a bridle
over the horse's head and jumped onto its
back. It bucked and kicked like crazy at
first, but he clung on until it got tired and
recognised him as master.

story continues on page 34

Now he could fly, Bellerophon made his battle plans. He armed himself with a bow and arrows, a spear and a lump of lead and took off to scout for his prey. By following the trail of smoke and ashes, he found the dreaded Chimera snoozing on a rock in the bright midday sunshine.

Pegasus carefully steered round behind it and swooped down to allow Bellerophon to fire stinging arrows into the monster's back. It woke with a start. Seconds later, a jet of red-hot fire came fizzing upwards. Pegasus dodged and Bellerophon leaned over closer to the beast's jaws.

Cloudy Home
Mount Olympus, the home of the gods, is a real mountain in Greece. Its top is often covered by clouds, making it creepy and mysterious.

Almost fainting with the heat, he stuck the lead on the point of his spear and shoved it down the Chimera's throat. The monster's fire melted the metal, which trickled down and gave it deadly tummy ache. The pain was more than it could stand and, with one last horrible flaming roar, it died.

Thunderman
The Greeks didn't understand thunder and lightning. They said flashes of lightning were thunderbolts thrown down by Zeus, whose name means "bright".

Bellerophon was now a star. He flew around the country on Pegasus giving air displays and getting more and more big-headed. Forgetting pride always comes before a fall, he even boasted he could ride to the top of Mount Olympus.

Sky Diver
Bellerophon's tumble from the skies gives us our expression "pride comes before a fall".

When Zeus saw Pegasus flapping towards him with a man on its back, he sent a bee to sting the horse's bottom. The animal reared up and threw its proud rider, who landed heavily in a thorn bush, breaking his leg and scratching out his eyes. Blind and lame, Bellerophon wandered the earth all alone for the rest of his days.

TOUGH TALK

All words in italics, e.g. *souls,* have their own explanation.

Heaven
The home of gods, goddesses and the *souls* of people who have led good lives. The Greek heaven was called the Elysian fields.

Immortal
A living thing that can never die or be killed.

Labyrinth
An ancient Cretan word for a maze, still used in English.

Legend
A story that has grown up around a heroic figure (who may have been a real person), or event (that may have actually taken place).

Nymph
A beautiful female *spirit* who guards the natural world. Some nymphs watch over hills and mountains, others over trees, forests, rivers and oceans.

Oracle
A place where priests or priestesses pass on advice or commands from the gods. Many ancient oracles claimed that they could foretell the future.

Prophet or **Prophetess**
Someone who foretells the future.

Ritual
A set of holy actions which form part of religious worship. Many important events in our lives, such as birth, marriage and death, are marked by rituals.

Sacred
The most important parts of a religion; anything that is holy.

Sacrifice
A ritual offering to a god or goddess to thank them for their help, or to ask for their future support. In the ancient world, the gift was often a human or animal victim.

Soul
The part of a creature that thinks and feels. Ancient peoples believed that the soul was *immortal,* and that when a person or creature died, their soul went to *heaven* or the *Underworld.*

Spirit
A living being that has no body. Spirit can also mean the *soul* of a creature.

Underworld
The home of dead *souls,* thought to be a land below the earth.

WHO'S WHO

A guide to the hottest names in Greek and Roman myth and legend. All names in capitals, e.g. HERCULES, have their own explanation.

Adonis (*ah–doh-niss*)
A young man so drop-dead gorgeous that he bowled over the goddess of love herself.

Unfortunately, the god of war wanted the goddess of love all for himself. So he turned into a wild boar and killed poor Adonis while he was out hunting.

Agamemnon (*agg-ah-mem-non*)
The king of Mycenae, who led the Greek army during the Trojan War. But while he was away fighting, his wife CLYTEMNESTRA kept herself busy with a new lover.

When Agamemnon arrived home, Clytemnestra and her lover killed him while he was splashing about in the bath.

Agamemnon was worshipped at ancient Mycenae, but there is no proof that the golden masks found there (*above*) actually belonged to him.

Ajax (*ay-jacks*)
One of the heroes in the Greek army at Troy. He was only slightly less brave than Achilles, and the two were best mates. After Achilles was killed by Paris, Ajax wanted to keep his old chum's armour.

But the armour was given to Odysseus instead. Ajax went berserk and ended up killing himself by falling on his sword.

Alcestis (*al-sess-tiss*)
Alcestis' husband was told that he could become immortal if he could find someone to die in his place. Only Alcestis loved him enough to offer herself.

Amazons (*am-ah-zonz*)
A race of female warriors who lived near the Black Sea. The Amazons used men as slaves for having children with and for doing the housework. Their queen, Hippolyta, (*bottom*) was ARES' daughter.

Andromeda (*ann-drom-ed-ah*)
Andromeda's mother boasted that her daughter was more beautiful than the sea god's servants. The sea god was furious, and sent a sea serpent to eat them. Andromeda was chained to a rock as a tasty bite for the monster, but Perseus whisked her away just in time.

phrodite (*afro-die-tea*)
he Greek goddess of love and
eauty, she was called Venus
y the Romans. She could
ake anyone fall in love.

pollo (*ah-poll-oh*)
he Greek god of healing,
oetry and music. His temple
t Delphi was home to the
ost famous oracle in Greece.

rachne (*ah-rack-knee*)
rachne stupidly dared to
hallenge the goddess ATHENE
o a weaving contest. In her
apestry, she showed the gods
s weak and dishonest beings.
thene was so angry that she
urned Arachne into a spider,
oomed to spin forever (*centre*).

res (*air-ease*)
he Greek god of war, called
Mars by the Romans. A bit
loodthirsty, he wasn't much
liked by other
gods.

Argonauts (*ah-go-noughts*)
The group of heroes, led by
Jason, who sailed in the *Argo*
to capture the Golden Fleece
(a shiny bit of sheepskin).

Artemis (*art-em-miss*)
The Greek goddess of hunting,
called Diana by the Romans.
She had a stinking temper –
when one hunter spotted her
bathing naked, she turned him
into a deer. Soon after, he was
caught and torn to pieces by
his own hunting dogs.

Athene (*a-thee-knee*)
The Greek goddess of wisdom,
called Minerva by the Romans.
She helped many heroes, such
as Perseus and Bellerophon.

Atlas (*at-lass*)
A TITAN who led a war against
the gods. The gods won, and
as a punishment Atlas was
sent to the end of the world
and forced to carry the sky on
his shoulders. The Atlas
mountains in northwest Africa
are named after him.

Castor and Pollux
These twin heroes sailed with
the ARGONAUTS. The group of

stars known as "gemini", or
the twins, are named after them.

Charon (*ka-ron*)
The ferryman who took the
dead across the River Styx to
the underworld (*bottom left*).
    The Greeks placed a coin in
the mouths of their dead to
pay Charon for his services.

Clytemnestra (*kly-tem-ness-trah*)
Clytemnestra and her lover
murdered her husband
AGAMEMNON when he
returned from the Trojan War.
    They waited until he was in
the bath then threw a net over
him and chopped him up with
an axe. Later, her son killed
her and her lover in revenge
for his father's death.

Cronos (*crow-noss*)
Cronos was the king of the

TITANS. He swallowed his kids
because he was terrified they
would destroy him.
    But Cronos' wife tricked
him into swallowing a rock
instead of his son ZEUS (*above*).
Later, Zeus killed Cronos. He
cut open his belly, and out
popped his brothers and sisters.

Cyclops (*sy-klops*)
Three giant brothers who had just one eye, smack in the middle of their foreheads.

Demeter (*der-me-ter*)
The Greek goddess of corn and mother of PROSERPINA. Called Ceres by the Romans.

Dionysus (*die-oh-nice-us*)
The swinging Greek god of wine and parties, known as Bacchus to the Romans.

Echo (*ekko*)
A nymph who helped ZEUS by chatting to his wife HERA while he was with his lovers.
   When Hera found out, she punished Echo by only letting her repeat, or "echo", what other people had said.

Eros (*ear-ross*)
The young Greek god of love, known as Cupid to the Romans.

Eros (*left*) was said to fire gold-tipped arrows at people, to make them fall in love.

Gorgons (*gore-gonz*)
The three gorgons were gruesome sisters with snakes for hair and bodies covered in scales and tusks. Their stares were so hideous that they turned people to stone.

Hades (*hay-dees*)
The moody Greek god of the underworld and the brother of ZEUS. He was known as Pluto to the Romans.

Harpies (*harp-ease*)
Female monsters that were birds with human faces. If anybody disappeared, the Greeks blamed the Harpies.

Hecate (*heh-ka–tea*)
The Greek goddess of darkness and magic. She was linked with the moon (*top right*).

Helios (*heel-lee-oss*)
A TITAN and god of the sun. Every morning he grabbed the sun, put it in his chariot, and galloped across the sky (*left*).

Hephaestus (*heff-east-us*)
The Greek god of fire, called Vulcan by the Romans.

Hera (*here-ah*)
The wife of ZEUS, Hera was the goddess of marriage and mothers. She is called Juno by the Romans.

Hercules (*her-cue-leaze*)
The Roman name for the Greek hero Heracles, son of the god ZEUS. He was famous for the twelve labours he had to perform after killing his children in a mad fit.

Hermes (*her-meaze*)
The Greek messenger god, called Mercury by the Romans. He is famous for his winged sandals, which let him fly.

Janus (*jane-us*)
The Roman god of doorways. He has two faces – one that looks back, the other that looks forward. January, the first month of the year, is named after him.

Mithras (*myth-rass*)
An Iranian god who became very popular with the Romans. Bull sacrifice was an important part of his religion (like the ancient Cretan religion, *centre*)

Narcissus (*nar-siss-us*)
When the nymph ECHO fell hopelessly in love with vain Narcissus, he just ignored her until she faded away with grief. ARTEMIS punished him by making him fall in love with his own reflection.

Unable to grab his image in the pool of water, he died of a broken heart (*above*). He was turned into the lovely flower that is named after him.

Odysseus (*oh-dee-see-us*)
A Greek hero who fought at Troy (*right*), he was known for his cunning. He thought up the idea of the wooden horse. But because he had angered the sea god POSEIDON, it took him ten years to get back home.

Orion (*oar-eye-on*)
Orion was a giant hunter with the power to walk across the sea. When ARTEMIS fell in love with him, jealous APOLLO tricked her by challenging her to hit a tiny speck out at sea. It was Orion! In her grief, Artemis turned him into a set of stars.

Pan
The Greek god of wild nature, he was famous for playing his pipes. His ability to make people feel suddenly scared gives us the word "panic".

Poseidon (*poss-eye-don*)
The Greek god of the sea, horses and earthquakes, called Neptune by the Romans.

Proserpina (*pro-sir-pee-nah*)
HADES carried Proserpina down into the underworld. Her mother DEMETER was so unhappy that Proserpina was allowed to spend spring with her, filling the world with flowers. When she stayed with Hades, it became winter.

Pygmalion (*pig-male-lee-on*)
This king of Cyprus carved a statue out of ivory and fell in love with it. APHRODITE felt sorry for him and turned the statue into a real woman.

Sirens (*sy-renz*)
Like the HARPIES, the sirens were part-woman and part-bird. They lured sailors to their death on the rocks with their beautiful singing.

Titans (*tie-tans*)
The titans were the first Greek gods. They were challenged by the children of the titan CRONOS, led by ZEUS. This battle lasted for ten years. Finally, the new gods won, and the titans were sent to live in the Underworld.

Uranus (*you-rain-us*)
Uranus was a TITAN and the first god of the sky, but he was defeated by his son CRONOS.

Zeus (*zyoos*)
Zeus was the Greek king of the gods, and was called Jupiter by the Romans. He used crashing thunderbolts to defeat his enemies.

INDEX

*The main stories for each name are in **bold**.*